MW00366329

You, the Viewer at Home, Moon

You, the Viewer at Home, Moon

Tom Will

maximus books

First paperback edition 2022
Copyright © 2022 by Tom Will

All rights reserved. No part of this book may be reproduced or transmitted in any form or by any means whatsoever without express written permission from the author, except in the case of brief quotations embodied in critical articles and reviews. Please refer all pertinent questions to the publisher.

Full colophon in back

I would like to especially thank Humphrey, Everett, Adam, Brendan, Hayden, Anna, Alan, Michael, Mother, Father, Family, Trout, Lydia, Stephanie, Frank, Wesley, Vincent, Roy, John, Danny, Buster, Charles, Tennessee, North Carolina, South Carolina, Virginia, West Virginia, Kentucky, Modelo, Camel, Bench, Notebook, Maximus. And also Matisse, Manray, Sappho, Catullus, Ezra, Toyota, Edna, Orion and Manhattan (the drink, not the place).

Contents

Moons

Decorous

My poetry will have the same fixtures as the rooms of my thoughts
A mansion with many rooms; rooms for each
Of me to walk around with rooms to
Walk around me

June, Once

A luna moth almost
Landed on your tongue
The special green color
Of special green running shoes
Still damp from being left
On the covered porch, all night, in
June

June is the best month
For luna moths the
Letters resemble
Each other

Luna-June
Moon-Spoon

The luna moth is on a
White square column
Is breathing with slow
Bellows-wings

Is like Frank O'hara said:

"We are breathing
Between each other"

Moth and me
Moon and you
Loon and June

All growing on the white square column like
Special green mushrooms, find them
In June

June, Twice

June fireworks
Echoing, lack of decay
In the time between gen-teel
The first vowels arriving, the
Heel and toe of
Vowels in gravel
The report can be confused
For afternoon thunder
On a clouded day, no proof
That a storm will come
But might pass, an afternoon
Sleeping sound with a woman
And reaching towards her
In and out of some dream
The same pair of hands
You closed the store with, lock it
And look down at her
That door
Soon the fireworks
Will be on sale
Gradually
The fireworks
Will be on sale
By the roadside
If you wake up in July

4

Easter Sunday

No shade or shadow on the soccer fields at noon; nothing
Except the goal posts at ends; and their lurid orange nets
No league took down the nets all winter; no league mends them
No league minds that purple flowers spring up in the net's shadow
Like the fisherman casting out too far into the sea at noon
Only to dredge up netfuls of purple flowers; imagine their surprise
At this; they swore the nets had come up empty the flowers were
    so light
Enough to feed great crowds; these netfuls of purple flowers;
    enough
To feed children and women and men; here come the ships now
With nets full of flowers; walking on the water

Fahey Brand Turtle Food

I smoke one cigarette a week because it tightens a little tightrope in my mind specifically it tunes the rope to a D note. One time I smoked a second cigarette it was odd the tightrope became a chorus of tightropes it became the open strings of a guitar opened to DADFAD but I was not careful with that tuning and became it. Sometimes open D minor will make you a turtle on the center line of a two-lane blacktop which is warm but a car ran me over and it sounded like running over a guitar.

Cocktail

All the widows of the world have liquorlogged cherries in between their teeth those holding handfuls of maraschino cherries ginlogged on Monday Wednesday Thursday and Saturday ryelogged on Tuesdays and Ryedays and red vestments in ordinary time on Sundays. If Dali were alive today he'd be pulled over for a beater Mitsubishi Eclipse full of maraschino cherries our new century is red and sweet and falling into small hands not suited to cherry holding. Proud commune maidens carrying breastfuls of syrup cherries in their blouses skirts and between breasts. The men wade into vats of cherries the men like sundials under a red sun the cherries like virgins bleeding virgin syrup. Cherries aborted and kept in jars a mockery without context. Satanists shave their faces and receive the Eucharist for black cherry Masses mockery with far too much context. Scientists are finding cherries in the deep sea salt this is why it is getting pinker redder really. Pinker is getting redder really. Jackie O ass against the floor back against the slouch of a wall in a hospital room licking her fingers clean of you guessed it.

All Winter Long

A few snakes freeze half-in and half-out of their pond water, and we will make our beds anew of winter.

Canoe

I think of our past lives
Only a blue sunless morning
Only the river coming and going
Into our canoe

In a way I can regard
Only as uncaring

Diesel

I am a kin to diesel. I am at sea level. I am at street level. I am at ear level to your engine. I am a confidant to all particles isolated in death's round chambers. I am a car for all to decay in. In all honesty. I am a piston for all diesel. I am a confessor for diesel's last confession. I ask diesel where it heard that dirty poem. In a bar. Where it heard that dirty joke. In a darker bar. I learned that diesel only hears dirty things in darker places. Diesel leaves me its possessions and effects. I am at street level, outside, breathing in diesel light. I am a piston for testate diesel, in all persons, honesty. If I become unseamed I can always hide in my friend diesel's truck bed, it was left to me.

June, again, July

Late June and
Walking so fast
You see the bellies
Of your wrists
Beneath the trees'
Un-tanned under-wrists

New Job

A row of flags sewn along the seams of my new
    Light jeans
Small triangular flags of the car dealership variety
    Tethering novelty
Made poorly, quickly, cheaply, latticing apart like prayer flags
    From previous tenants
And now I am going to begin to start running

Fuel Injection

American Mental Teen
Imagining coffee in Cuba
Con Chicarro all noon

While you hold a moka pot
Big enough to be buried in
And consider carburetors a sin

Easter Sunday, Greek Orthodox

There are lessons I have forgotten but not the teachers, so that the teachers are the lessons, entirely: first spring the azaleas, then gone, then the rosebushes, then gone, then the magnolias, then gone, or; say the TH- through your S-, or the S- through your TH-; or a Sunday that looks as if it were a Sunday that I heard a lesson in, a homily when I was younger; a quiet Sunday with no alarms so the volunteer firemen drive the fire engines to the store for groceries.

Ice Cream Cones in Naples

Neapolitan cats
Dripping onto the street corners
Each head scoop sized
Chocolates
Vanillas
Strawberries
Licking itself
Licking itself
Feral licks

Theremin

I woke to the singing of schoolchildren
"Let All Mortal Flesh Keep Silence"
And the rest of the day
In sole remembrance of my dream
One child's voice trebled in sole
Relief; a theremin in a park
Neither understanding the other

The Need For Trees In Rain

The smoker's tan that is my left forearm
In old age will not leave you
Or lead you astray or tarnish not true rust
Ours aluminum fencing sheets of waves in
Oh how lovely is the rain in the waves of our fence
The tide of our fence the need for trees
In rain the need for trees
In rain

Houses cannot catch fire in our rain
It's a lie told by urban leagues
But the need for trees in headlights
The need for wet pavement
Basements cold and wet
The need for your bare hands
That slept off the bed gloved by our window unit air
    conditioner
They gave me what sleeping outside gave me
And cannot leave me
The need for trees in rain

Go West

I am to go west to west-america
I heard a noise like a car-crash
Hubcaps rolled out east-to me

The cars here are small and kept together
In an attempt at preserving warmth

So I am to go warm to west-america
Go west, to see the icebergs form
Drift eastward and shrink into clouds

Lake Cumberland, Gethsemane

Crawling up the lakeshore steps, Christlike, soundless
The man broke both his legs jumping into the water

They broke instantly because the water was so cold
So unfrozen, so clear, broken as the mount of olives

Crawling up the lakeshore steps, Christlike, soundless
He wonders "Did any of this make any sound at all?"

Lake's Lonely Offices

It is a terrible office
And I do not envy
The man representing
The Army Core of Engineers
Going *cove* to *core*
Tellingly, telling
Each fern
Each shore
Each false shore of leaves in the water
Each dredged ladderstep
Each tongue of limestone
Each Fibonacci lip at the rivermouth
Turned lake
A change like cove to core
Is such a basic abridgment
Is in the handwriting
Is a reader's digest of the full novel of the river
And this man had the short grassy straw
To tell them all, telling each thing
That the river must become a lake, must be lowered
In a house-boat tone of voice
A tone of somewhat ashamed ambition
60 feet, or else Nashville may flood

A Flight With No Meal

The coal of ego is
Glowing in a dangerous
Place

As we all try to
Exit the aircraft

That horrible coal
To say and be clever but

They all just want to go
Home

To their favorite bar
Where its tender's tongue
Is glowing

Givenchy Aviators

My hair tapping the glass aquarium of my sunglasses I am a lobster tank to scare and delight children's hands we are all together at the seashore for dinner my hair is children with hands of hair and fingers of hair and lobster whiskers it's a lie the children tapping the glass does not give me a headache the highway is sunny and empty I am a lonely lobster in a tank in a doctor's office.

Tide

A girl has pierced eyelashes the piercings are very small and look very much like extensions of the lashes because the metal is so dark when woven so lightly

A girl has pierced eyes the metal ring is very small and goes through each pupil like the faint rings of a distant planet

A girl has pierced toes and must wear open-toed shoes she is very strong and can be supported from the ceiling by the feet if you run fishing wire through the piercings

She may have more piercings but I just cannot be sure

Cherries In Season

My orchid flower's
Stem stem stems
Are cherry stems
Stem one and all

The cherries
In the flower's throats
A cocktail
For the streets at night

The freckles
Only girls can have
Cannot be feigned
Or hid with tears

Like cherries in a jar jar jar
Below the skin my orchid grows

Two Mirrors

Two Chinese mothers walking in a park hands clasped for walking masks and wrapped glasses color coordinated one in pink gloves the other in pink leggings.

I don't have any idea what they are saying and if I did then you wouldn't be able to peel the separate things away like clothes the trees the leaves the sky the park the whole curtain and rod of 2:15 PM in late March that lets them go beyond.

They are going beyond into a black peaceful vacuum where they will continue to walk and clasp hands behinds their backs and wear pink accents against a black background of space.

Devils

There are as many devils as there can be footsteps of rain

Well, half as many

Here comes one, two, three, over the parsley now

Sharing a Bed

My feet
Our cold

Lawns at Night

Lawns at night, an American flag made of Christmas lights, a fountain lit up like the moon at night, my soul too is louder at night, my soul too is a fountain, the tall church lit up at night like the moon over a dark neighborhood's trees, trees without names at night like the subjects of a historical capitol city who lived and died nameless in the shadow of a tall church that is now lit up at night, the flower shop is closed at 12:20 AM and the flowers are each in their very own windows, the flower shop is full of Grace Kelly's silhouettes, emerald green at night, NO OUTLET signs lit up in my headlights like the moon at night, the firing range's stations all lit up with floodlights, the shell casings lit up from the moon because the moon came out again tonight.

Crime Scene #1

A wasp's nest was alive tonight
In the corner of your alley

Alive with light red yellow
Green from the combs
Light-falling dandruff

Crime Scene #2

All possible TV colors from the cop car
Blue red from beyond the cemetery entrance
That they've blocked off green
In the morning grass after something happened

Inside the cop car it is night time
Inside the cemetery grounds it is morning still as
The victim's family demands the rights of citizenship

They claim that to die inside the cemetery walls is citizenship
For all their heirs thereafter into the Red Blue Green

Crime Scene #3

Groucho Marx cuckoo clock
The eyebrows shrug
On the hours
The cigar burns on
The hours
Ash on the A frame's mantle
Dusty old fishing lures
And the break action casts a rainbow
Through its chrome
Onto the wall
Shaped like a fish scale
I want you to look through
A freshly oiled gun barrel
See the Jacob's Ladder inside
Rainbows with wedding bands
For wings
Bullets seeking angels
Like God perhaps tomorrow
A smug click like
Your friend's mother's teeth
I want you to look
Through a freshly oiled gun barrel
Sometime

Crime Scene #4

There is a house illuminated by headlights for the first time
And second you walk by an electric scooter tall as the fence it
    was left on
And third you walk by a knee high nonelectric scooter with
    hockey pucks for wheels
Made of metal that looks like it would melt if you touched it
Both are painted the same abandoned green color
I am full of foreboding like a class of children being walked
    along a red rope
Being walked past a driveway blocked with yellow caution
    tape
Where are the adults taking these children I wonder
One of the children is left handed and holding the rope in
    his right hand
Because they are all holding the rope in their right hand
But later on he forgets that this happened

Leaves in Shade

Pure leaves resting out of the sun
Huddled together faithfully
They are not refugees
They are not animals
They are not a carton of eggs
They are simply waiting at the bar

August Pool

Swimming under the lanes in the pool that are train tracks. Rowing across an older film. The train depot is in between. Deep and shallow. Young and old. Work and play. Is this too obvious inside the pool? Then it is twenty times more obvious walking past the fences twenty years later in winter when the pool is covered in film stock. The public pool is a tableau film of the sphinx's riddle to man, of man. A bald man kissed for too long, violated his age, his role in the tableau of the pool.

And how still the pool becomes for fifteen minutes every hour, as the tableau expands into the showers and the grass and eventually bicycles.

Tempera

Only one more night, as
A bouquet of dead flowers

Blue, the kind between
Larkspur and Gatorade

And good thing too, something
Brushed by me last night

And I realized I was
Brittle and hard to see

And I had hoped my sentiments
Were clearer

And more lasting

Next week I will be
A poet again

Car Crash

It looked like the car
Was playing charades
Last night
And tried to act out
"Praying Mantis"
For the people inside

Plane Crash

The black box
Is a black cube
Walked around by death
Like a Mecca

My Many Neighbors

My neighbors' televisions are radios for me in the bathtub because I am crouching up against the shiny metal and using them for molars and suddenly their lives are as clear to my mouth as a bell.

Early Fall

Oh
To be somewhat a poet
Or to be
Leaves gathered
In the crook
Of a neck
Of a rooftop
Or to be
Oh
A neat stack
Of dewy shingles
Oh
To be of early fall

Sled Poem

When I am snoring
I dream your little neck
My voice is stupid but honest
As you slide down my nose
Sledding down the 4 AM hills
In your aluminum trash can lid
I dream your little necklace
On your little neck
Made from the last of the trash can lids

42

That Pair of Jeans is Crosseyed

I want a denim burial, a denim death mask, a denim tomb-
stone because I decided one day years ago to have Shoulders
And Calves And Yes Even one of those too, and that old pair of
jeans is my life and not any other and is turning cockeyed at the
hips and knees. I don't think the cemetery or the trees would
mind, would you? Not with the right belt. That Dylan shade of
blue is just right, is just right, old photo blue; lapis lazuli with
the original button fly because I always liked when you did the
buttons all back up.

MOONS

The Moon, Try #3

The moon swaying
Like a traffic light
In the wind

Seems to say
Slow down
Slow down

Eclipse Moon

The moon has always been tarred
The moon has always been feathered
But tonight the car is driving fast enough
That all the feathers fly into the backseat

Buster Keaton Moon

The moon was always wearing black face
The moon was always wearing white face

Dimly Moon

I unrolled the front windows
When the rain lets down
To a less than intermittent setting
On the wipers

Now put your arm out the window
And the water from the wheels
And the pavement is whisking
At you moon, dimly

And when we get home
I love to turn on
All the lights in the house
Because it gets too dark

Pearl Moon

Spraying canned air on our underarms and groins.

Drying like paint as it blows across the moon.

When we made love; it sounded like someone was dragging a string of pearls down the road.

Cockroach on the Moon

A cockroach in the grass seems happier than a cockroach on the moon; but nobody asked them to be everywhere.

Not one single married couple sees their dust in the honey-moon suite's nightlight.

Nobody sees them as the villa's tiled roof; or antennae flecks of stucco.

Obsessive Moon Sounds

The way a hot pan waits for you
To leave the room

You, the Viewer at Home, Moon

A night so quiet my spit striking the pavement sounds like snapping fingers. A night so quiet I can hear death's traffic far off into death's stadium its vuvuzelas half a mile off its drums and brave sections that I should walk towards you in.

I want to reveal my brilliance in its turnings to you but have no almanac for turnings no birth chart for brilliance no way to determine peak brilliance as I hear the stadium so full of lights.

Leather Moon

Moonless Nights
Leather Shadows
Leather Halls
The Leather Clad Objects
In My House
Each A Slide
For Slide Projectors

Fentanyl Moon

I never touch the stuff
But I sure do think
About the moon
Like dirty snow

Like a fentanyl patch
The nurse stole off the shoulder
Of a cancer patient
Chewing like gum

Show and Tell Moon All Night

Someone is going to pick me up. Not my parents, not my parent's friends that live close by or my one-time girlfriend with a car at sixteen. But someone is going to pick me up from school and drive me home. I'll sit in the front seat for the whole forty-five minutes, so I'll leave my Walkman with you.

When they pick me up, I'll play the radio playing Maroon Five. Who all the girls sing to at parties, like a chorus of frogs or raindancing Indians. A rain dance making it rain would have been less surprising than seeing a bossa nova song make every girl in a basement sing in unison without spilling a single red drop of root beer.

It's the winter solstice and the moon is already out. It's on every station. They don't sing along to any other song that comes on that night. It's the last school-day before Christmas break. All of this is in a duffel bag under the stairs in the main building named after a saint.

Moretta Moon

Its silence defeats my poem
The married dentist defeats my tooth
The leotarded female thief cracks the safe
Easily, her nails are a compass circling my window's mansion
The new moon stole the full moon from my safe, from my
    bedroom mansion's safe
The final act of the heist poem is one hundred women fleeing,
    matching dark hair, all masked
Teeth hidden
The crime was so popular how could I press charges
It was so dark, nobody saw a thing

Wonder Bread Moon

She is the only person I know that could spread cold butter over wonder bread without tearing it, and she does not love me anymore.

The Newish Ritual of Hope–Severance Moon

Another woman escaped from your harem
One less leg vein for your bypass
And in rare amputetic form
The moon is four months pregnant

Irregular Anna Taylor-Joy Moon Sonnet

How can the clouds move behind the half moon
If this was a sonnet I'd repeat this
Question fourteen times
Pausing before the ninth line
If I was famous for my poems and
If I met that one famous actress
At a gala I could just see the roles
She was in like a television screen
(Here I trail off; note the clouds still moving)
Like television screens in all the corners of
The sports bar playing all of her roles and
That is how the moon seems to me tonight
The clouds still drifting in right behind it

Dove on the Moon

What a dove, made of lead, sees on the moon, made of silver, nestling down, in a soft crater, he looks to me, to be a teardrop.

Wine Moon

Watching you gone by
I am a pair of nostril moons
Waiting to breathe
As your mouth drinks
From the bottle

Sistine Chapel Moon

Orion is reaching out to the moon
The moon is reaching out to Orion
Like God and Man in the Sistine Chapel
With all the other figures played by crows

Crows
On the rooftops hopped into hypermuscular poses
Some Old Testament figures; some new
Some figures undetermined

Crows
In undetermined poses
With their beaks held open to the moon
On the rooftops; on the mossless chimneys
Only on the dying wood; they avoid any speck of moss

The crows becoming Michelangelo's detractors
Hoping they cursed him with an impossible commission
How wrong they still are; cackling all night

In Cold Blood Moon

My mustache tastes of cigarettes
An egg with salt, alone in the moon
I wake up three days distanced from you
Your lassos of hair bowering me, bird alone
My room lassoed, a red balloon in the shower lassoed
My three days of loneliness walking the state fair alone
All things lassoed, your hair wrapped around my big toe
Like a red balloon, in cold blood in the moon

Kentucky Moon

I think that the moon itself is hid
Like lottery tickets
In the sneakers
Strung up along the telephone poles

Death Premonition Moon

Ketchup only tastes like vinegar anymore
And I sit against every light pole I see
O virgin moon, half-sleeping in the traincar with me

Geriatric Moon

The moon wears its shirt backwards buttoned
Because I take care of its washing up
And hes no longer proud of his meals
His cock is just a series of rivulets
Of violins in space

Hungry Moon

I ate a hamburger so cold my teeth hurt
And drove the car all night as you slept
And the moon wasn't there; I ate that too

Published by Maximus Books in the USA

ISBN: 978-0-578-29110-9 (paper)

Text set in Sabon Next and Mrs. Eaves

Artwork: front cover, half title, frontispiece, 16, 30, 44, *Mothtail 1–5*, © 2022 by Brendan McCauley; back cover, *Moon Jar from Joseon Dynasty*, 17th c., Art Institute of Chicago.

The following poems originally appeared, in one form or another, in the following publications:

Apocalypse Confidential: "Crime Scenes 1-3," "Cocktail," "A Flight with No Meal," "Fahey Brand Turtle Food," "Leaves in Shade," "Lake Cumberland Gethsemane," "Plane Crash," and "In Cold Blood Moon"

The Crank: "Dove on The Moon"

Door is a Jar Magazine: "The Moon Try #3"

Expat: "Geriatric Moon"

Maximus Magazine: "Show and Tell Moon All Night" and "Pearl Moon"

Misery Tourism: "Car Crash"

Olney Magazine: "Diesel" and "Cherries in Season"

Rejection Letters: "My Many Neighbors" and "Tide"

Safety Propaganda: "Fentanyl Moon" and "Buster Keaton Moon"

Tragickal: "Givenchy Aviators," "Two Mirrors," and "Wonder Bread Moon," and "August Pool"

Version 9 Magazine: "Easter Sunday," "Crime Scene #4," "Sled Poem," "All Winter Long," and "You, The Viewer At Home Moon"

About the author

Tom Will's poems have appeared in *Expat Press*, *Rejection Letters*, *Misery Tourism*, *Safety Propaganda*, *Tragickal*, *Door is a Jar Magazine*, *Version 9 Magazine*, *Olney Magazine*, *The Crank,* and *Maximus Magazine*. His first book, *Sonnet Cycle*, was published by Schism Neuronics. He lives in Tennessee and is the poetry editor at *Apocalypse Confidential*.

CPSIA information can be obtained
at www.ICGtesting.com
Printed in the USA
BVHW071418090622
639350BV00005B/146

9 780578 291109